Blackstone Outdoor Gas Griddle Cookbook for Beginners

Amazingly Tasty, Quick and Easy Recipes for Your Outdoor Flat Top Gas Grill

Deasa Woodam

© Copyright 2020 Deasa Woodam - All Rights Reserved.

In no way is it legal to reproduce, duplicate, or transmit any part of this document by either electronic means or in printed format. Recording of this publication is strictly prohibited, and any storage of this material is not allowed unless with written permission from the publisher. All rights reserved.

The information provided herein is stated to be truthful and consistent, in that any liability, regarding inattention or otherwise, by any usage or abuse of any policies, processes, or directions contained within is the solitary and complete responsibility of the recipient reader. Under no circumstances will any legal liability or blame be held against the publisher for any reparation, damages, or monetary loss due to the information herein, either directly or indirectly.

Respective authors own all copyrights not held by the publisher.

Legal Notice:

This book is copyright protected. This is only for personal use. You cannot amend, distribute, sell, use, quote or paraphrase any part of the content within this book without the consent of the author or copyright owner. Legal action will be pursued if this is breached.

Disclaimer Notice:

Please note the information contained within this document is for educational and entertainment purposes only. Every attempt has been made to provide accurate, up-to-date and reliable, complete information. No warranties of any kind are expressed or implied. Readers acknowledge that the author is not engaging in the rendering of legal, financial, medical or professional advice.

By reading this document, the reader agrees that under no circumstances are we responsible for any losses, direct or indirect, which are incurred as a result of the use of information contained within this document, including, but not limited to, errors, omissions, or inaccuracies.

Table of Contents

Introduction 6
Chapter 1: Blackstone Outdoor Gas Griddle 7
    What is Griddle Seasoning? 7
    Blackstone Griddle Seasoning Method 8
    Griddle Tools 9
    Griddling Secrets 10
    Care and Maintenance 11
Chapter 2: Breakfast 13
    Healthy Oatmeal Pancakes 13
    French Toast 14
    Strawberry Pancakes 15
    Delicious Blueberry Pancakes 16
    Healthy Banana Pancakes 17
    Nutritious Tofu Spinach Scramble 18
    Easy Scrambled Egg 19
    Tomato Spinach Egg Scramble 20
    Dijon Tofu Scramble 21
    Creamy Scrambled Egg 22
    Cheese Cinnamon Pancakes 23
    Tofu Veggie Scramble 24
    Feta Cheese Omelet 25
    Italian Egg Scrambled 26
    Greek Omelet 27
Chapter 3: Poultry 28
    Lemon Herb Chicken 28
    Delicious Chicken Kebab 30
    BBQ Chicken Tenders 31
    Pesto Chicken & Asparagus 32
    Flavorful Chicken Kebabs 33
    Spicy Chicken 34
    Turkey Patties 35
    Turkey Spinach Burgers 36

Spicy Turkey Patties 37
Greek Chicken Breast 38
Tasty Chicken Skewers 39
Marinated Chicken Skewers 40
Marinated Chicken Breast 42
Delicious Chicken Fritters 43
Yummy Turkey Burger Patties 44

Chapter 4: Beef, Pork & Lamb 45
Delicious Pork Patties 45
Steak Tips 46
Tasty Beef Kebabs 47
Lemon Pepper Tenderloin 48
Spicy Lamb Chops 49
Greek Lamb Kebabs 50
Flavorful Lamb Patties 51
Beef Herb Patties 52
Delicious Beef Kofta 53
Pork Kebabs 54
Delicious Burger Patties 55
Rosemary Pork Chops 56
Ground Beef 57
Easy Picadillo 58
Italian Pork Chops 59

Chapter 5: Fish & Seafood 60
Simple Salmon Patties 60
Mustard Tuna Patties 61
Mahi Mahi Fish Fillets 62
Easy & Tasty Salmon 63
Spicy Shrimp 64
Cajun Shrimp Skewers 65
Lemon Garlic Halibut 66
Tasty Tuna Cakes 67
Greek Tuna Patties 68
Sauteed Shrimp 70

Chapter 6: Vegetables & Side Dishes 71
    Mushrooms & Green Beans 71
    Mushroom Cauliflower Rice 72
    Sauteed Zucchini 73
    Tasty Cauliflower Wedges 74
    Brussel Sprouts Skewers 75
    Lemon Zucchini Stir Fry 76
    Veggie Tofu Stir Fry 77
    Healthy Spinach Cauliflower Rice 78
    Mushrooms & Asparagus 79
    Zucchini Noodles 80

Chapter 7: Snacks 81
    Healthy Broccoli Cheese Patties 81
    Cheese Broccoli Fritters 82
    Cajun Broccoli Patties 83
    Chicken Patties 84
    Tasty Turkey Patties 85
    Parmesan Zucchini Patties 86
    Cheese Broccoli Fritters 87
    Italian Broccoli Fritters 88
    Parmesan Cauliflower Cakes 89
    Sweet Potato Patties 90

Chapter 8: Game Recipes 91
    Easy & Tasty Cornish Hens 91
    Lemon Orange Cornish Hen 92
    Delicious Cornish Hen 93
    Herb Cornish Hen 94
    Rosemary Butter Hen 95

Conclusion 96

Introduction

If you think outdoor backyard parties then the Blackstone outdoor gas griddle is one of the best cooking appliances available in the market. The Blackstone is one of the old and trusted griddle manufacturers popular in the USA for their outdoor griddling appliances. It is capable to cook a large quantity of food into a single cooking batch. The Blackstone griddle is available in two different sizes one is 28 inch and the other is a 36-inch model. The griddle is made up of quality stainless steel material and it comes with a black powder coating.

The large size H-shape burners come with a separate controller knob you can operate them with different temperature settings as per your cooking needs. The Blackstone griddle uses a propane gas cylinder for griddle fuel. The flat-top griddles cook your food using the conduction principle to cook your food by transferring the heat from the hot surface to direct into your food. Due to this technique, your food is not in direct contact with a gas flame and makes your food juicer instead of dried. The Blackstone griddle is portable and lightweight to use outdoor cooking. It is easily fitted into the trunk of the car and carry one place to another to make perfect weekend camping.

The book contains 80 tasty and mouth-watering griddle recipes that come from different categories like breakfast, poultry, beef, pork & seafood, vegetables & side dishes, snacks, and game recipes. The recipes written in this cookbook are unique and written into easily understandable form with their preparation and cooking time. All the recipes contain step by step instruction set which makes your cooking process easy. The recipes written in this book are ended with their nutritional value information. The nutritional value information will help to keep track of daily calorie intake. There are various books available in the market thanks for choosing my book. I hope you love and enjoy all the griddle recipes written in this cookbook.

Chapter 1: Blackstone Outdoor Gas Griddle

The Blackstone outdoor gas griddle is one of the best gas griddle cooking appliances available in the market. The Blackstone outdoor griddle is mainly available in two cooking sizes. One is 28 inches and another is 36 inches to cook lots of food in a single cooking cycle. The Blackstone gas griddle is made up of stainless steel material and comes with a black powder coating. The black powder coating protects your griddle from rust. The topmost cooking surface area is made up of thick rolled steel material. The 28-inch gas griddle is loaded with two H-shape gas burners which cover the 470 sq. inch flat cooking surface area. The single burner of the griddle is capable to produce 15000 BTU heat whereas both the burners same time produces 30000 BTU heat to cook your food faster and evenly. The 36-inch gas griddle is loaded with 4 H-shape burners which cover a 720 sq. inch cooking surface area. This griddle is ideal for outdoor parties, family dinners, and more. The 4 burners together produce the 60000 BTU heat. These gas burners are equipped with a separate control switch so you can easily operate only those burners where you place the food for cooking.

The griddle comes with a battery-operated ignition system so you just need to push the ignition switch and turn the gas controller to start the gas burners. It is capable to produce the maximum heat (350 °F) to cook your favorite food over a griddle cooking surface. The griddle comes with a propane tank holder and two side-mounted shelves to hold your oil bottles and other cooking essentials. To move the griddle easily from one place to another it comes with 4 caster wheels.

When you think about weekend parties or get together dinner parties then Blackstone gas griddle is one of the best choices for you. It is capable to cook a large quantity of food, you can cook 28 hamburgers, 16 steaks, and 72 hot dogs into a single cooking batch. You can cook all this food at the same time but at different temperatures by just adjusting the controller switch as per recipe needs.

What is Griddle Seasoning?

Seasoning is the process to prepare your griddle cooking surface area for cooking. There are two reasons behind the seasoning process.

1. To coat your griddle cooking surface area to prevent rust.

2. Seasoning helps to create permanent non-stick cooking surface area naturally.

Seasoning is one of the important and essential steps done before using your Blackstone griddle for cooking purposes. When you season the griddle, it will give you the best cooking results and it also helps to increase the lifespan of your Blackstone gas griddle.

Blackstone Griddle Seasoning Method

Before starting the actual cooking process, you must season your griddle using the following step-by-step guide. The following seasoning steps not only protect the gas griddle from rusting but also help to improve the cooling efficiency.

1. To prevent rust and any damage over the cooking surface area your Blackstone gas griddle comes with a pre-seasoned state. To use the griddle the first time you need to wash the cooking surface area using soapy water (This is the first and last time you have to use soapy water to clean your griddle). After washing the cooking surface dry it properly by using a paper towel.
2. After drying the cooking surface turn on all the controller knob to set gas burners at maximum temperature settings for 10 to 15 minutes until you have noticed that the griddle top surface starts brown and discolor.
3. After finishing step 2 pour the little cooking oil over the griddle surface. You can use your favorite oil like coconut oil, olive oil, vegetable oil, and more to season the surface area of your griddle. After pouring some oil over the griddle surface use a paper towel to spread the oil equally over the griddle surface area. It is also recommended to use high quality cast iron conditioner for coating the griddle surface area.
4. Turn on all the knob and set it to its maximum temperature settings for 15 to 30 minutes. After some time the cooking surface area turns black color and the oil starts smoking because the griddle temperature reaches its smoking point. After some time the oil smoke disappears completely.
5. After finishing step 4 turn off your griddle and allow it to cool down for 10 minutes. Repeat this seasoning process again and again until you have noticed the cooking surface of the griddle turns brown. You can repeat step 3 and step 4 for at least 3 to 4 repetitions.

6. Finally, you need to wipe the griddle surface area by using high quality cooking oil or it is recommended to use cast iron conditioner spray for coating your griddle surface area to prevent oxidation.
7. Finally, the Blackstone griddle seasoning process completes successfully and your griddle is ready for outdoor cooking.

Griddle Tools

- Scraper tool

The scraper is one kind of sharp and durable stainless steel blade having a handle with grip to give perfect control over griddle surface. These tools are mostly used to scrapping, digging, and clean the griddle surface area for derbies.

- Spatula

The spatula is a broad and flat stainless steel blade comes with a grip handle. It is a necessary tool to use for flipping, spreading, and mixing purposes and lift your food like omelets, burgers, pancakes, and more. It is available in three sizes-small, medium, and large you can choose your spatula as per your cooking needs.

- Squeeze bottle

Squeeze bottles are one of the best tools to squeeze oil, water, and sausage over the griddle while cooking your food. You can store healthy oils in the bottle and use it easily as per your cooking needs. You can also use water squeeze bottles to create the steam for certain recipes and it is also used to clean the griddle surface for derbies.

- Grill press tool

The concept behind using a grill press tool is to keep your foot flat on the griddle surface and even distribution of heat. It is made from cast iron material and comes with easy to hold handle with a wooden grip. While making burgers you can use this tool to remove the excess grease out from your burgers.

- Basting Covers

Basting covers are made from stainless steel material or aluminum material available in round and square shape having the handle to hold the cover. The basting covers are used in some recipes to steam vegetables, for melting cheese, and more.

Griddling Secrets

1. Use healthy cooking oils

When cooking food on your griddle you need oil. Choose healthy oil options like olive oil, avocado oil, coconut oil, vegetable oil, peanut oil, butter, sesame oil, and more.

2. Use the right accessories

To get perfect cooking results you need to use the right accessories to handle your food. There are three essential tools like a spatula to flip your food, a scraper to clean the griddle, and squeeze bottles for oil and water that are needed while griddling your food. You can also use extra tools like grill press and basting covers. Basting covers help to melting cheese and steaming your veggies.

3. Prepare your ingredients

Before starting the actual cooking process make sure you have prepared all the things ready for your cooking because the griddle surface area is very hot and cooks your food faster. You don't have enough time to prepare ingredients and monitor your food at the same time.

4. Use water while cooking

Water is essential while cooking your food with steam. The steam helps to cook your food faster without losing the flavors. The squeeze water bottles are the perfect tool for adding the water for steaming.

5. Preheat your griddle

Before starting cooking preheat your griddle at medium temperature settings to burn the oils present over your griddle surface.

6. Select the best temperature settings

The best temperature settings depend on what kind of food you want to cook on a griddle.

- High heat: This setting is an ideal choice for cooking lean meat or searing purpose only.
- Medium heat: This setting is an ideal choice for cooking seafood, eggs, hamburgers, pancakes, toasting bread, and more.
- Low heat: Using these settings you can cook fatty meats.

7. Use meat thermometer

If you are a new user you don't get the idea that the meat piece is cooked perfectly from the inside. So you have to need a meat thermometer to check the internal temperature of your meat reaches its desire cooking point.

Care and Maintenance

- Valve check

Before checking the valves make sure the gas supply is off from the cylinder. Then push the gas controller knob and release the knob spring back to its original position. If not then change the valve assembly before using your griddle. Push the knob and turn it low position and again turn back to the off position to check whether the knob turns smoothly or not.

- General cleaning

General cleaning is necessary after each use. To clean plastic parts with the help of soapy water and wipe with a cloth. To the clean painted surface of the griddle use mild detergent, soapy water, and dry with a soft cloth. To clean the stainless steel surface using soapy water and dry cloth.

- Griddle cooking surface cleaning

After each use griddle starts season automatically and a thick non-stick layer is created over the surface. Do not use soapy water to clean the griddle surface.

Use little water to remove the rust with the help of a scraper and clean the surface with a dry paper towel.

If you find the rust spot over the griddle surface uses low grit sandpaper or steel wool to remove the rust spot.

When you finish the griddle cleaning coat a thin layer of oil spray over the griddle surface to prevent it from rusting.

- Storage and Maintenance

To extend the life of your griddle you have to cover it and store it in a dry place.

If the LP gas cylinder is connected to the griddle keep your appliance in the well-ventilated area keep it away from the reach of children.

Store the griddle indoor-only if the LP cylinder is disconnected from the griddle.

Chapter 2: Breakfast

Healthy Oatmeal Pancakes

Preparation Time: 10 minutes
Cooking Time: 15 minutes
Serve: 2

Ingredients:

- 1 egg
- 2 tbsp butter, melted
- 1/4 cup water
- 1/2 cup milk
- 1 1/2 cups cooked oatmeal
- 1 tsp baking powder
- 1/2 cup flour, gluten-free
- 1/2 tsp salt

Directions:

1. In a mixing bowl, whisk the egg with butter, water, milk, and oatmeal.
2. Add baking powder, flour, and salt and stir well to combine.
3. Preheat the griddle to high heat.
4. Spray griddle top with cooking spray.
5. Scoop batter onto the hot griddle top and cook for 2-3 minutes and flip pancake and cook for 3 minutes or until golden brown.
6. Serve and enjoy.

Nutritional Value (Amount per Serving):

- Calories 513
- Fat 19.3 g
- Carbohydrates 69.7 g
- Sugar 3.6 g
- Protein 16.2 g
- Cholesterol 117 mg

French Toast

Preparation Time: 10 minutes
Cooking Time: 10 minutes
Serve: 2

Ingredients:

- 2 eggs
- 5 bread slices
- 1/2 tbsp brown sugar
- 1/2 cup orange juice

Directions:

1. In a shallow dish, whisk eggs with brown sugar and orange juice.
2. Coat bread slices with egg mixture.
3. Preheat the griddle to high heat.
4. Spray griddle top with cooking spray.
5. Place bread slices onto the hot griddle top and cook for 2 minutes, flip and cook until golden brown.
6. Serve and enjoy.

Nutritional Value (Amount per Serving):

- Calories 159
- Fat 5.2 g
- Carbohydrates 20.4 g
- Sugar 8.7 g
- Protein 7.7 g
- Cholesterol 164 mg

Strawberry Pancakes

Preparation Time: 10 minutes
Cooking Time: 10 minutes
Serve: 2

Ingredients:

- 2 eggs
- 1 cup strawberries, diced
- 1 1/2 tsp baking powder
- 1/4 tsp baking soda
- 1/3 cup tapioca starch
- 1/2 cup potato starch
- 1 1/2 cups white rice flour
- 2 tbsp sugar
- 2 1/3 cups buttermilk
- 1/4 cup butter, melted
- 3/4 tsp salt

Directions:

1. In a bowl, whisk eggs with buttermilk and butter.
2. Add remaining ingredients and whisk until well combined.
3. Add strawberries and stir well. Let sit the mixture for 5 minutes.
4. Preheat the griddle to high heat.
5. Spray griddle top with cooking spray.
6. Scoop mixture onto the hot griddle top and cook for 1-2 minutes. Flip and cook until golden brown.
7. Serve and enjoy.

Nutritional Value (Amount per Serving):

- Calories 867
- Fat 25.1 g
- Carbohydrates 143.1 g
- Sugar 4 g
- Protein 29.6 g
- Cholesterol 20 mg

Delicious Blueberry Pancakes

Preparation Time: 10 minutes
Cooking Time: 10 minutes
Serve: 3

Ingredients:

- 2 eggs
- 1 cup blueberries
- 1/3 cup butter, melted
- 8 oz sour cream
- 1 1/2 cups milk
- 4 tsp baking powder
- 1/4 cup sugar
- 2 cups all-purpose flour
- 1/2 tsp salt

Directions:

1. In a mixing bowl, mix flour, baking powder, sugar, and salt. Set aside.
2. In a separate bowl, whisk eggs with butter, cream, and milk.
3. Pour egg mixture into the flour mixture and mix until well combined. Add blueberries and stir well.
4. Preheat the griddle to high heat.
5. Spray griddle top with cooking spray.
6. Scoop 1/4 cup mixture onto the hot griddle top and cook until golden brown from both sides.
7. Serve and enjoy.

Nutritional Value (Amount per Serving):

- Calories 449
- Fat 27.7 g
- Carbohydrates 44.7 g
- Sugar 27.5 g
- Protein 8.8 g
- Cholesterol 180 mg

Healthy Banana Pancakes

Preparation Time: 10 minutes
Cooking Time: 10 minutes
Serve: 4

Ingredients:

- 2 eggs
- 1/3 cup olive oil
- 2 cups of milk
- 2 ripe bananas, mashed
- 1 tsp cinnamon
- 1 tsp baking soda
- 1 tbsp baking powder
- 3 cups whole wheat flour
- 1 tsp salt

Directions:

1. In a mixing bowl, mix flour, baking soda, cinnamon, baking powder, and salt.
2. In a separate bowl, whisk eggs with oil, milk, and mashed bananas.
3. Add egg mixture into the flour and mix well.
4. Spray griddle top with cooking spray.
5. Scoop mixture onto the hot griddle top and cook for 2-3 minutes. Flip and cook until golden brown.
6. Serve and enjoy.

Nutritional Value (Amount per Serving):

- Calories 125
- Fat 11.4 g
- Carbohydrates 1 g
- Sugar 0.8 g
- Protein 5.8 g
- Cholesterol 164 mg

Nutritious Tofu Spinach Scramble

Preparation Time: 10 minutes
Cooking Time: 7 minutes
Serve: 2

Ingredients:

- 1/2 block firm tofu, crumbled
- 1/4 cup zucchini, chopped
- 1/4 tsp ground cumin
- 1 tbsp turmeric
- 1 cup spinach
- 1 tbsp olive oil
- 1 medium tomato, chopped
- Pepper
- Salt

Directions:

1. Preheat the griddle to medium heat.
2. Add oil on top of the griddle.
3. Add tomato, zucchini, and spinach and sauté for 2 minutes.
4. Add tofu, cumin, turmeric, pepper, and salt, and sauté for 5 minutes.
5. Serve and enjoy.

Nutritional Value (Amount per Serving):

- Calories 105
- Fat 8.6 g
- Carbohydrates 6.3 g
- Sugar 2.2 g
- Protein 3.6 g
- Cholesterol 0 mg

Easy Scrambled Egg

Preparation Time: 10 minutes
Cooking Time: 5 minutes
Serve: 2

Ingredients:

- 2 eggs, lightly beaten
- 1/2 tomato, chopped
- 1 tbsp olive oil
- 1/4 tsp garlic powder
- Pepper
- Salt

Directions:

1. Preheat the griddle to medium heat.
2. Add oil on top of the griddle.
3. Add tomatoes and cook until softened.
4. Whisk eggs with garlic powder, pepper, and salt.
5. Pour egg mixture on top of tomatoes and cook until eggs are set.
6. Serve and enjoy.

Nutritional Value (Amount per Serving):

- Calories 125
- Fat 11.4 g
- Carbohydrates 1 g
- Sugar 0.8 g
- Protein 5.8 g
- Cholesterol 164 mg

Tomato Spinach Egg Scramble

Preparation Time: 10 minutes
Cooking Time: 10 minutes
Serve: 2

Ingredients:

- 4 eggs
- 3 tomatoes, chopped
- 1 1/2 cups baby spinach, chopped
- 1/3 cup basil, chopped
- 1 tbsp olive oil
- Pepper
- Salt

Directions:

1. Preheat the griddle to medium heat.
2. Add oil on top of the griddle.
3. Add tomatoes and cook until softened.
4. Meanwhile, whisk eggs with basil, pepper, and salt.
5. Add spinach over tomatoes and cook until wilted.
6. Pour egg mixture over spinach and tomatoes and cook until eggs are set.
7. Serve and enjoy.

Nutritional Value (Amount per Serving):

- Calories 226
- Fat 16.2 g
- Carbohydrates 8.8 g
- Sugar 5.6 g
- Protein 13.5 g
- Cholesterol 327 mg

Dijon Tofu Scramble

Preparation Time: 10 minutes
Cooking Time: 10 minutes
Serve: 2

Ingredients:

- 8 oz extra-firm tofu, mash with a fork
- 1/3 cup almond milk
- 1/4 tsp onion powder
- 1/2 tsp garlic powder
- 1 tsp Dijon mustard
- 1/2 tsp paprika
- 1/2 tsp turmeric
- 2 tbsp nutritional yeast
- 1 tbsp butter
- 1/4 tsp salt

Directions:

1. In a bowl, mix nutritional yeast, onion powder, garlic powder, mustard, paprika, turmeric, and salt. Add milk and whisk well.
2. Preheat the griddle to high heat.
3. Melt butter on the hot griddle top.
4. Add tofu and stir until lightly browned.
5. Add the nutritional yeast mixture and mix well.
6. Cook until tofu absorbed all the liquid.
7. Serve and enjoy.

Nutritional Value (Amount per Serving):

- Calories 165
- Fat 9.6 g
- Carbohydrates 7.9 g
- Sugar 2.6 g
- Protein 14.5 g
- Cholesterol 5 mg

Creamy Scrambled Egg

Preparation Time: 10 minutes
Cooking Time: 5 minutes
Serve: 2

Ingredients:

- 4 eggs
- 2 tbsp heavy cream
- 1 tbsp butter
- 1/4 tsp cinnamon
- Pepper
- Salt

Directions:

1. In a bowl, whisk eggs and heavy cream.
2. Preheat the griddle to high heat.
3. Melt butter on the hot griddle top.
4. Add the egg mixture and stir until eggs are cooked.
5. Sprinkle with ground cinnamon.
6. Serve and enjoy.

Nutritional Value (Amount per Serving):

- Calories 185
- Fat 15 g
- Carbohydrates 1 g
- Sugar 1 g
- Protein 12 g
- Cholesterol 346 mg

Cheese Cinnamon Pancakes

Preparation Time: 10 minutes
Cooking Time: 10 minutes
Serve: 4

Ingredients:

- 4 eggs
- 1 tbsp butter, melted
- 1/2 tsp cinnamon
- 1/2 cup cream cheese
- 1/2 cup almond flour

Directions:

1. Add all ingredients except butter into the blender and blend until combined.
2. Preheat the griddle to medium heat.
3. Melt butter on the hot griddle top.
4. Scoop mixture onto the hot griddle top and cook for 2-3 minutes. Flip and cook until golden brown.
5. Serve and enjoy.

Nutritional Value (Amount per Serving):

- Calories 270
- Fat 24 g
- Carbohydrates 4 g
- Sugar 1 g
- Protein 10 g
- Cholesterol 201 mg

Tofu Veggie Scramble

Preparation Time: 10 minutes
Cooking Time: 7 minutes
Serve: 2

Ingredients:

- 1/2 block firm tofu, crumbled
- 1/4 cup zucchini, chopped
- 1 tbsp olive oil
- 1 tomato, chopped
- 1 tbsp chives, chopped
- 1 tbsp coriander, chopped
- 1/4 tsp ground cumin
- 1 tbsp turmeric
- 1 cup spinach
- Pepper
- Salt

Directions:

1. Preheat the griddle to high heat.
2. Add oil to the griddle top.
3. Add tomato, zucchini, and spinach and sauté for 2 minutes.
4. Add tofu, cumin, turmeric, pepper, and salt and sauté for 5 minutes.
5. Top with chives, and coriander.
6. Serve and enjoy.

Nutritional Value (Amount per Serving):

- Calories 102
- Fat 8.5 g
- Carbohydrates 5.1 g
- Sugar 1.4 g
- Protein 3.1 g
- Cholesterol 0 mg

Feta Cheese Omelet

Preparation Time: 10 minutes
Cooking Time: 5 minutes
Serve: 1

Ingredients:

- 3 eggs
- 1/2 tsp olive oil
- 2 tbsp feta cheese, crumbled
- 1/4 cup fresh mint, chopped
- 2 tbsp almond milk
- Pepper
- Salt

Directions:

1. In a bowl, whisk eggs with feta cheese, mint, milk, pepper, and salt.
2. Preheat the griddle to low heat.
3. Add oil to the griddle top.
4. Pour egg mixture on griddle top and cook until eggs are set.
5. Flip omelet and cook for 2 minutes more.
6. Serve and enjoy.

Nutritional Value (Amount per Serving):

- Calories 274
- Fat 20 g
- Carbohydrates 4 g
- Sugar 2 g
- Protein 20 g
- Cholesterol 505 mg

Italian Egg Scrambled

Preparation Time: 10 minutes
Cooking Time: 10 minutes
Serve: 2

Ingredients:

- 4 eggs
- 1 tbsp olive oil
- 1/4 tsp dried oregano
- 1/2 tbsp capers
- 3 olives, sliced
- 1/2 cup cherry tomatoes, sliced
- 2 tbsp green onions, sliced
- 1 bell pepper, diced
- Pepper
- Salt

Directions:

1. Preheat the griddle to medium heat.
2. Add oil to the griddle top.
3. Add green onions and bell pepper and cook until pepper is softened.
4. Add tomatoes, capers, and olives and cook for 1 minute.
5. Add eggs and stir until eggs are cooked.
6. Season with oregano, pepper, and salt.
7. Serve and enjoy.

Nutritional Value (Amount per Serving):

- Calories 230
- Fat 17 g
- Carbohydrates 8 g
- Sugar 5 g
- Protein 12 g
- Cholesterol 325 mg

Greek Omelet

Preparation Time: 10 minutes
Cooking Time: 5 minutes
Serve: 1

Ingredients:

- 4 eggs, beaten
- 1/4 tsp Italian seasoning
- 1/4 tsp dried oregano
- 1/4 cup mozzarella cheese, shredded
- 4 tomato slices
- Pepper
- Salt

Directions:

1. In a small bowl, whisk eggs with salt.
2. Preheat the griddle to medium heat.
3. Spray griddle top with cooking spray.
4. Pour egg mixture into the hot griddle top and cook until eggs are set. Sprinkle with oregano and Italian seasoning.
5. Arrange tomato slices on top of the omelet and sprinkle with cheese.
6. Cook omelet for 1-2 minutes.
7. Serve and enjoy.

Nutritional Value (Amount per Serving):

- Calories 284
- Fat 19 g
- Carbohydrates 4 g
- Sugar 3 g
- Protein 25 g
- Cholesterol 655 mg

Chapter 3: Poultry

Lemon Herb Chicken

Preparation Time: 10 minutes
Cooking Time: 12 minutes
Serve: 4

Ingredients:

- 1 1/2 lbs chicken breasts, skinless and boneless
- 1 tbsp red wine vinegar
- 3 tbsp olive oil
- 3 tbsp fresh lemon juice
- 1 tbsp garlic, minced
- 1/4 tsp cayenne pepper
- 1 tsp fresh thyme
- 1/2 tsp oregano
- 1/2 tsp pepper
- 1/2 tsp salt

Directions:

1. Add chicken into the zip-lock bag.
2. Pour remaining ingredients over chicken. Seal bag and shake well and place in the fridge for overnight.
3. Preheat the griddle to high heat.
4. Spray griddle top with cooking spray.
5. Place marinated chicken on hot griddle top and cook for 4-6 minutes on each side or until chicken is cooked.
6. Serve and enjoy.

Nutritional Value (Amount per Serving):

- Calories 425
- Fat 23 g
- Carbohydrates 1 g

- Sugar 0.3 g
- Protein 50 g
- Cholesterol 150 mg

Delicious Chicken Kebab

Preparation Time: 10 minutes
Cooking Time: 10 minutes
Serve: 4

Ingredients:

- 1 1/2 lbs chicken breast, boneless & cut into 1-inch pieces
- 1 tbsp olive oil
- 1/2 tsp pepper
- 1 tsp dried oregano
- 1 tbsp fresh lime juice
- 1/2 tsp sea salt

Directions:

1. Add chicken into the bowl.
2. Add remaining ingredients over chicken and mix well and place in the fridge overnight.
3. Preheat the griddle to medium heat.
4. Spray griddle top with cooking spray.
5. Thread marinated chicken onto the skewers.
6. Place chicken skewers onto the hot griddle top and cook for 8-10 minutes.
7. Serve and enjoy.

Nutritional Value (Amount per Serving):

- Calories 225
- Fat 7.8 g
- Carbohydrates 1.3 g
- Sugar 0.2 g
- Protein 36.2 g
- Cholesterol 109 mg

BBQ Chicken Tenders

Preparation Time: 10 minutes
Cooking Time: 15 minutes
Serve: 4

Ingredients:

- 1 1/2 lbs chicken tenders
- 2 tbsp BBQ sauce
- 1 tsp poultry seasoning
- 1 tbsp olive oil
- Pepper
- Salt

Directions:

1. Add all ingredients except oil in a zip-lock bag. Seal bag and place in the refrigerator for 2 hours.
2. Preheat the griddle to high heat.
3. Add oil on top of the griddle.
4. Place marinated chicken tenders on the hot griddle top and cook until lightly browned and cooked.
5. Serve and enjoy.

Nutritional Value (Amount per Serving):

- Calories 365
- Fat 15 g
- Carbohydrates 3 g
- Sugar 2 g
- Protein 50 g
- Cholesterol 150 mg

Pesto Chicken & Asparagus

Preparation Time: 10 minutes
Cooking Time: 25 minutes
Serve: 3

Ingredients:

- 1 lb chicken thighs, skinless, boneless, and cut into strips
- 1 1/2 cups cherry tomatoes, halved
- 1/4 cup basil pesto
- 1 lb asparagus, ends trimmed and cut in half
- 2 tbsp olive oil

Directions:

1. Preheat the griddle to medium heat.
2. Add oil on top of the griddle.
3. Place chicken on hot griddle top and season with salt and cook for 5-8 minutes or until chicken is cooked.
4. Add pesto and asparagus and cook for 2-3 minutes.
5. Add tomatoes and stir well and serve.

Nutritional Value (Amount per Serving):

- Calories 405
- Fat 20.7 g
- Carbohydrates 7.3 g
- Sugar 1.2 g
- Protein 47 g
- Cholesterol 135 mg

Flavorful Chicken Kebabs

Preparation Time: 10 minutes
Cooking Time: 14 minutes
Serve: 6

Ingredients:

- 2 lbs chicken thighs, cut into pieces
- 1 yellow bell pepper, cut into medium pieces
- 1 green bell pepper, cut into medium pieces
- 2 tbsp olive oil
- 3 garlic cloves, minced
- 1 tsp dried oregano
- 1 red bell pepper, cut into medium pieces
- 2 tbsp soy sauce

Directions:

1. Add chicken and remaining ingredients into the bowl and mix well. Cover and place in the refrigerator overnight.
2. Preheat the griddle to medium-high heat.
3. Thread marinated chicken pieces and bell pepper pieces onto the skewers.
4. Place skewers onto the hot griddle top and cooks for 7 minutes on each side.
5. Serve and enjoy.

Nutritional Value (Amount per Serving):

- Calories 355
- Fat 16 g
- Carbohydrates 5.6 g
- Sugar 3 g
- Protein 44 g
- Cholesterol 135 mg

Spicy Chicken

Preparation Time: 10 minutes
Cooking Time: 12 minutes
Serve: 4

Ingredients:

- 4 chicken breasts
- 1/2 tsp smoked paprika
- 1/2 tsp ground coriander
- 1 tsp ground cumin
- 1 tsp garlic powder
- 1/4 tsp black pepper
- 2 tbsp olive oil
- 1/2 tsp sea salt

Directions:

1. Preheat the griddle to medium-high heat.
2. In a small bowl, mix garlic powder, oil, pepper, paprika, coriander, cumin, and salt and rub all over the chicken.
3. Place chicken on hot griddle top and cook for 4-6 minutes on each side.
4. Serve and enjoy.

Nutritional Value (Amount per Serving):

- Calories 345
- Fat 18 g
- Carbohydrates 1 g
- Sugar 0.2 g
- Protein 42.5 g
- Cholesterol 130 mg

Turkey Patties

Preparation Time: 10 minutes
Cooking Time: 8 minutes
Serve: 5

Ingredients:

- 1 lb ground turkey
- 1/3 cup bacon, chopped
- 1/3 cup green onions, chopped
- 1 cup cheddar cheese, shredded
- 1/4 cup BBQ sauce
- 1/2 tsp garlic powder
- Pepper
- Salt

Directions:

1. Add ground turkey and remaining ingredients into the bowl and mix until well combined.
2. Preheat the griddle to medium-high heat.
3. Make patties from meat mixture and place on a hot griddle top and cook for 4 minutes on each side.
4. Serve and enjoy.

Nutritional Value (Amount per Serving):

- Calories 291
- Fat 17 g
- Carbohydrates 5 g
- Sugar 3.6 g
- Protein 30.6 g
- Cholesterol 116 mg

Turkey Spinach Burgers

Preparation Time: 10 minutes
Cooking Time: 10 minutes
Serve: 4

Ingredients:

- 1 lb ground turkey
- 1 tbsp almond flour
- 1/4 tsp crushed red pepper
- 1 tsp parsley
- 1/2 cup baby spinach, chopped
- 1/2 tsp pepper
- 1 tsp oregano
- 1 tsp garlic powder
- 1/3 cup sun-dried tomatoes
- 1/2 cup feta cheese, crumbled
- 1/2 tsp sea salt

Directions:

1. Add all ingredients into the bowl and mix until just combined.
2. Make patties from the mixture.
3. Preheat the griddle to high heat.
4. Place patties on hot griddle and cook for 3-5 minutes on each side.
5. Serve and enjoy.

Nutritional Value (Amount per Serving):

- Calories 290
- Fat 17.4 g
- Carbohydrates 2.9 g
- Sugar 1.4 g
- Protein 34.5 g
- Cholesterol 132 mg

Spicy Turkey Patties

Preparation Time: 10 minutes
Cooking Time: 10 minutes
Serve: 2

Ingredients:

- 1/2-pound ground turkey
- 1/2 tsp cumin
- 1/2 tsp paprika
- 1 tbsp cilantro, chopped
- 1/2 lime juice
- 1/2 shallot, peeled and minced
- 1/2 jalapeno pepper
- 1/2 tsp pepper
- 1/2 tsp sea salt

Directions:

1. Add ground turkey, spices, herbs, and lime juice in mixing bowl and mix well until combine.
2. Preheat the griddle to medium-high heat.
3. Spray griddle top with cooking spray.
4. Make patties from meat mixture and place onto the hot griddle top and cook for 5 minutes on each side.
5. Serve and enjoy.

Nutritional Value (Amount per Serving):

- Calories 232
- Fat 12.7 g
- Carbohydrates 2.4 g
- Sugar 0.4 g
- Protein 31.4 g
- Cholesterol 116 mg

Greek Chicken Breast

Preparation Time: 10 minutes
Cooking Time: 20 minutes
Serve: 4

Ingredients:

- 4 chicken breasts, skinless and boneless
- 1 tbsp dried oregano
- 1 tbsp ginger garlic paste
- 1/4 cup lemon juice
- 1/4 cup olive oil
- 1/2 tsp paprika
- 1 tsp dried parsley
- 1 tsp dried thyme
- 1 tsp dried rosemary
- 1/4 tsp pepper
- 1 tsp salt

Directions:

1. Add all ingredients except chicken to the bowl and mix well.
2. Add chicken to the bowl and coat well and place it in the refrigerator for 1 hour.
3. Preheat the griddle to medium-high heat.
4. Spray griddle top with cooking spray.
5. Place marinated chicken on hot griddle and cook for 6-7 minutes on each side or until cooked through.
6. Slice and serve.

Nutritional Value (Amount per Serving):

- Calories 402
- Fat 24 g
- Carbohydrates 2.4 g
- Sugar 0.4 g
- Protein 42.8 g
- Cholesterol 130 mg

Tasty Chicken Skewers

Preparation Time: 10 minutes
Cooking Time: 10 minutes
Serve: 4

Ingredients:

- 1 lb chicken breast, boneless, skinless, and cut into ¾-inch cubes
- 1 tbsp rosemary, minced
- 1 tbsp oregano, minced
- 1/2 tsp red chili flakes, crushed
- 2 garlic cloves, minced
- 1 tbsp fresh lemon juice
- 2 cups green seedless grapes, rinsed
- 1 tsp lemon zest
- 1/4 cup olive oil
- 1/2 tsp salt

Directions:

1. Thread chicken pieces and grapes onto the skewers and place skewers on the plate.
2. In a small bowl, mix together lemon juice, lemon zest, rosemary, oregano, chili flakes, garlic, oil, and salt, and pour over chicken skewers.
3. Place chicken skewers into the refrigerator overnight.
4. Preheat the griddle to high heat.
5. Spray griddle top with cooking spray.
6. Place marinated chicken skewers onto the hot griddle top and cook for 3-5 minutes on each side.
7. Serve and enjoy.

Nutritional Value (Amount per Serving):

- Calories 278
- Fat 15.9 g
- Carbohydrates 9.8 g
- Sugar 7.7 g
- Protein 24.6 g
- Cholesterol 73 mg

Marinated Chicken Skewers

Preparation Time: 10 minutes
Cooking Time: 20 minutes
Serve: 2

Ingredients:

- 1 1/2 lbs chicken breast, cut into 1-inch cubes
- For marinade:
- 1 tbsp red wine vinegar
- 5 garlic cloves
- 1/2 cup lemon juice
- 1/4 tsp cayenne
- 1 cup olive oil
- 1/2 cup yogurt
- 2 tbsp fresh rosemary, chopped
- 2 tbsp dried oregano
- 1/4 cup fresh mint leaves
- Pepper
- Salt

Directions:

1. Add all marinade ingredients into the blender and blend until smooth.
2. Pour marinade into a large bowl.
3. Add chicken to the bowl and coat well and place in the refrigerator for 1 hour.
4. Preheat the griddle to high heat.
5. Spray griddle top with cooking spray.
6. Remove marinated chicken from the refrigerator and slide onto the skewers.
7. Place chicken skewers onto the hot griddle top and cook for 3-5 minutes on each side.
8. Serve and enjoy.

Nutritional Value (Amount per Serving):

- Calories 677

- Fat 55.8 g
- Carbohydrates 7.1 g
- Sugar 3 g
- Protein 38.8 g
- Cholesterol 111 mg

Marinated Chicken Breast

Preparation Time: 10 minutes
Cooking Time: 14 minutes
Serve: 4

Ingredients:

- 2 lbs chicken breasts, skinless and boneless
- 1 tbsp garlic, minced
- 3 tbsp olive oil
- 1 tbsp balsamic vinegar
- 2 tbsp fresh lemon juice
- 1/2 tsp pepper
- 1/2 tsp onion powder
- 1/2 tsp red pepper flakes
- 1 tsp dried oregano
- 1/2 tsp kosher salt

Directions:

1. Add all ingredients into the zip-lock bag. Seal bag and place in refrigerator overnight.
2. Preheat the griddle to medium-high heat.
3. Spray griddle top with cooking spray.
4. Place marinated chicken on hot griddle and cook for 5-7 minutes.
5. Flip chicken to other side and cook for 5-7 minutes.
6. Slice and serve.

Nutritional Value (Amount per Serving):

- Calories 530
- Fat 27.5 g
- Carbohydrates 1.7 g
- Sugar 0.4 g
- Protein 65.9 g
- Cholesterol 202 mg

Delicious Chicken Fritters

Preparation Time: 10 minutes
Cooking Time: 10 minutes
Serve: 4

Ingredients:

- 1 lb ground turkey
- 1/2 cup breadcrumbs
- 1 tsp onion powder
- 1 tsp garlic powder
- 1/2 cup parmesan cheese, shredded
- Pepper
- Salt

Directions:

1. Add all ingredients into the bowl and mix until just combined.
2. Make patties from the mixture.
3. Preheat the griddle to high heat.
4. Spray griddle top with cooking spray.
5. Place patties on hot griddle and cook for 4-5 minutes on each side.
6. Serve and enjoy.

Nutritional Value (Amount per Serving):

- Calories 312
- Fat 11.6 g
- Carbohydrates 11.8 g
- Sugar 1.3 g
- Protein 38.6 g
- Cholesterol 109 mg

Yummy Turkey Burger Patties

Preparation Time: 10 minutes
Cooking Time: 10 minutes
Serve: 9

Ingredients:

- 1 egg, lightly beaten
- 1 lb ground turkey
- 2 tbsp cilantro, chopped
- 1/2 tsp garlic, minced
- 1/3 cup breadcrumbs
- 1 tsp Creole seasoning
- 2 tbsp lemon juice
- Pepper
- Salt

Directions:

1. Add all ingredients into the bowl and mix until just combined.
2. Make patties from the mixture.
3. Preheat the griddle to high heat.
4. Spray griddle top with cooking spray.
5. Place patties on hot griddle and cook until patties are golden brown from both sides.
6. Serve and enjoy.

Nutritional Value (Amount per Serving):

- Calories 125
- Fat 6.3 g
- Carbohydrates 3.1 g
- Sugar 0.4 g
- Protein 15 g
- Cholesterol 70 mg

Chapter 4: Beef, Pork & Lamb

Delicious Pork Patties

Preparation Time: 10 minutes
Cooking Time: 10 minutes
Serve: 4

Ingredients:

- 1 lb ground pork
- 1/2 tsp ground cumin
- 1/2 tsp coriander
- 1/2 tsp dried thyme
- 1 tsp paprika
- 1 tsp garlic powder
- 1 tsp onion powder
- Pepper
- Salt

Directions:

1. Add all ingredients into the bowl and mix until well combined.
2. Preheat the griddle to high heat.
3. Spray griddle top with cooking spray.
4. Make patties from the meat mixture and place onto the hot griddle top and cook until golden brown from both sides.
5. Serve and enjoy.

Nutritional Value (Amount per Serving):

- Calories 169
- Fat 4.1 g
- Carbohydrates 1.5 g
- Sugar 0.4 g
- Protein 30 g
- Cholesterol 83 mg

Steak Tips

Preparation Time: 10 minutes
Cooking Time: 5 minutes
Serve: 3

Ingredients:

- 1 lb steak, cut into cubes
- 1 tsp Montreal steak seasoning
- 1 tsp olive oil
- Pepper
- Salt

Directions:

1. In a bowl, add steak cubes and remaining ingredients and toss well.
2. Preheat the griddle to medium-low heat.
3. Spray griddle top with cooking spray.
4. Add the meat onto the hot griddle top and stir fry until cooked.
5. Serve and enjoy.

Nutritional Value (Amount per Serving):

- Calories 315
- Fat 9.1 g
- Carbohydrates 0 g
- Sugar 0 g
- Protein 54.6 g
- Cholesterol 136 mg

Tasty Beef Kebabs

Preparation Time: 10 minutes
Cooking Time: 15 minutes
Serve: 4

Ingredients:

- 1 lb ground beef
- 1/2 tsp cayenne
- 1/2 tsp turmeric
- 1 tbsp ginger garlic paste
- 1/4 cup cilantro, chopped
- 1/2 cup onion, minced
- 1/4 tsp ground cinnamon
- 1/4 tsp ground cardamom
- 1 tsp salt

Directions:

1. Add meat and remaining ingredients into the bowl and mix until well combined.
2. Preheat the griddle to high heat.
3. Spray griddle top with cooking spray.
4. Make sausage shape kebabs and place them onto the hot griddle top and cook for 10-15 minutes. Turn kebabs halfway through.
5. Serve and enjoy.

Nutritional Value (Amount per Serving):

- Calories 226
- Fat 7.4 g
- Carbohydrates 2.6 g
- Sugar 0.7 g
- Protein 34.9 g
- Cholesterol 101 mg

Lemon Pepper Tenderloin

Preparation Time: 10 minutes
Cooking Time: 20 minutes
Serve: 6

Ingredients:

- 2 lbs pork tenderloin
- 1 tsp fresh lemon juice
- 2 tbsp olive oil
- 1 garlic clove, minced
- 1 tsp fresh parsley, minced
- 1/2 tsp kosher salt

Directions:

1. Add all ingredients except pork tenderloin into the zip-lock bag and mix well.
2. Add pork tenderloin zip-lock bag. Seal bag and place in the fridge overnight.
3. Preheat the griddle to medium-high heat.
4. Spray griddle top with cooking spray.
5. Place pork tenderloin on hot griddle top and cook for 15-20 minutes.
6. Slice and serve.

Nutritional Value (Amount per Serving):

- Calories 255
- Fat 10 g
- Carbohydrates 0.2 g
- Sugar 0 g
- Protein 39.6 g
- Cholesterol 110 mg

Spicy Lamb Chops

Preparation Time: 10 minutes
Cooking Time: 10 minutes
Serve: 6

Ingredients:

- 12 lamb chops, trim excess fat
- For rub:
- 1 tbsp turmeric powder
- 1/2 tsp ground coriander
- 1 tbsp chili powder
- 1 tsp kosher salt

Directions:

1. Preheat the griddle to medium-high heat.
2. Spray griddle top with cooking spray.
3. In a small bowl, mix ground coriander, chili powder, turmeric, and salt and rub all over lamb chops.
4. Place lamb chops on hot griddle top and cook for 3-5 minutes on each side or until cooked.
5. Serve and enjoy.

Nutritional Value (Amount per Serving):

- Calories 645
- Fat 52 g
- Carbohydrates 1.4 g
- Sugar 0.1 g
- Protein 38 g
- Cholesterol 160 mg

Greek Lamb Kebabs

Preparation Time: 10 minutes
Cooking Time: 10 minutes
Serve: 6

Ingredients:

- 1 1/2 lbs Lamb, cut into 2-inch pieces
- 1/8 tsp red pepper flakes
- 1 lemon zest, grated
- 1 tbsp garlic, minced
- 2 tsp fresh oregano, chopped
- 5 tbsp olive oil
- 1 1/2 tbsp fresh parsley, chopped
- 1 1/2 tbsp fresh mint leaves, chopped
- 1 1/2 tbsp fresh rosemary, chopped
- 1 1/2 tsp pepper
- 1 tsp kosher salt

Directions:

1. Add lamb chunks and remaining ingredients into the zip-lock bag. Seal bag and place in the fridge overnight.
2. Preheat the griddle to medium-high heat.
3. Spray griddle top with cooking spray.
4. Thread marinated lamb chunks onto the skewers.
5. Place skewers onto the hot griddle top and cook for 8-10 minutes.
6. Serve and enjoy.

Nutritional Value (Amount per Serving):

- Calories 320
- Fat 20.2 g
- Carbohydrates 2.1 g
- Sugar 0.1 g
- Protein 32.2 g
- Cholesterol 102 mg

Flavorful Lamb Patties

Preparation Time: 10 minutes
Cooking Time: 15 minutes
Serve: 4

Ingredients:

- 1 lb ground lamb
- 1/4 tsp cayenne pepper
- 1/2 tsp ground allspice
- 1 tsp ground cinnamon
- 1 tsp ground coriander
- 1 tsp ground cumin
- 1/4 cup fresh parsley, chopped
- 1/4 cup onion, minced
- 1 tbsp garlic, minced
- 1/4 tsp pepper
- 1 tsp kosher salt

Directions:

1. Add all ingredients into the large bowl and mix until well combined.
2. Preheat the griddle to high heat.
3. Spray griddle top with cooking spray.
4. Make patties from meat mixture and place onto the hot griddle top and cook for 4-5 minutes on each side.
5. Serve and enjoy.

Nutritional Value (Amount per Serving):

- Calories 225
- Fat 8.5 g
- Carbohydrates 2.6 g
- Sugar 0.4 g
- Protein 32.3 g
- Cholesterol 102 mg

Beef Herb Patties

Preparation Time: 10 minutes
Cooking Time: 8 minutes
Serve: 5

Ingredients:

- 1 egg, lightly beaten
- 1 lb ground beef
- 2 tbsp fresh parsley, chopped
- 1 tsp dry oregano
- 1 tsp dry mint
- 3 tbsp breadcrumbs
- 1 small onion, grated
- Pepper
- Salt

Directions:

1. Add all ingredients into the bowl and mix until combined.
2. Preheat the griddle to high heat.
3. Spray griddle top with cooking spray.
4. Make patties from the meat mixture and place them onto the hot griddle top and cook for 4-5 minutes on each side.
5. Serve and enjoy.

Nutritional Value (Amount per Serving):

- Calories 285
- Fat 15 g
- Carbohydrates 5.3 g
- Sugar 1.3 g
- Protein 32.5 g
- Cholesterol 114 mg

Delicious Beef Kofta

Preparation Time: 10 minutes
Cooking Time: 10 minutes
Serve: 8

Ingredients:

- 2 lbs ground beef
- 4 garlic cloves, minced
- 1 onion, minced
- 2 tsp cumin
- 1 cup fresh parsley, chopped
- 1/4 tsp pepper
- 1 tsp salt

Directions:

1. Add all ingredients into the bowl and mix until just combined.
2. Preheat the griddle to high heat.
3. Spray griddle top with cooking spray.
4. Shape meat mixture into the kabab shapes and place onto the hot griddle top and cook for 4-6 minutes on each side.
5. Serve and enjoy.

Nutritional Value (Amount per Serving):

- Calories 225
- Fat 7.3 g
- Carbohydrates 2.5 g
- Sugar 0.7 g
- Protein 35 g
- Cholesterol 101 mg

Pork Kebabs

Preparation Time: 10 minutes
Cooking Time: 15 minutes
Serve: 2

Ingredients:

- 1 lb pork tenderloin, cut into 1-inch pieces
- 1 tbsp Italian seasoning
- 1 onion, cut into 1-inch pieces
- 2 tbsp olive oil
- 1/2 tsp paprika
- 1/2 tsp oregano
- 1/2 tsp garlic powder
- Pepper
- Salt

Directions:

1. In a bowl, add all ingredients and mix well and place in the fridge overnight.
2. Preheat the griddle to high heat.
3. Spray griddle top with cooking spray.
4. Thread marinated pork pieces and onion pieces onto the skewers.
5. Place skewers onto the hot griddle top and cook for 15 minutes. Turn skewers after every 3-4 minutes.
6. Serve and enjoy.

Nutritional Value (Amount per Serving):

- Calories 490
- Fat 24.2 g
- Carbohydrates 7 g
- Sugar 3.2 g
- Protein 60.2 g
- Cholesterol 170 mg

Delicious Burger Patties

Preparation Time: 10 minutes
Cooking Time: 10 minutes
Serve: 6

Ingredients:

- 1 lb ground beef
- 1 lb ground lamb
- 1/2 cup green onion, chopped
- 2 tbsp olive oil
- 1 tsp dried rosemary
- 1 tsp pepper
- 1 tbsp dried oregano
- 1 tbsp dried thyme
- 1 tsp cumin
- 1 1/2 tsp salt

Directions:

1. Add all ingredients into the large bowl and mix until well combined.
2. Preheat the griddle to high heat.
3. Spray griddle top with cooking spray.
4. Make patties from the meat mixture and place onto the hot griddle top and cook for 5 minutes on each side.
5. Serve and enjoy.

Nutritional Value (Amount per Serving):

- Calories 331
- Fat 15.2 g
- Carbohydrates 1.9 g
- Sugar 0.2 g
- Protein 44.5 g
- Cholesterol 136 mg

Rosemary Pork Chops

Preparation Time: 10 minutes
Cooking Time: 15 minutes
Serve: 4

Ingredients:

- 4 pork chops, boneless
- 1 tbsp olive oil
- 1 tsp dried rosemary, crushed
- 1/4 tsp pepper
- 1/4 tsp sea salt

Directions:

1. Season pork chops with pepper and salt.
2. Mix oil and rosemary and rub all over pork chops.
3. Preheat the griddle to high heat.
4. Place pork chops onto the hot griddle top and cook pork chops from both sides until completely done.
5. Serve and enjoy.

Nutritional Value (Amount per Serving):

- Calories 260
- Fat 19.9 g
- Carbohydrates 1 g
- Sugar 0 g
- Protein 18.1 g
- Cholesterol 69 mg

Ground Beef

Preparation Time: 10 minutes
Cooking Time: 8 minutes
Serve: 4

Ingredients:

- 1 lb ground beef
- 2 garlic cloves, minced
- 1 tbsp olive oil
- 3 tbsp green onion, sliced
- 2 1/2 tbsp soy sauce
- 1/2 tsp stevia drops
- 1 tsp red pepper, crushed
- 1/2 tsp fresh ginger, minced

Directions:

1. Preheat the griddle to medium heat.
2. Add oil to the griddle top.
3. Add garlic and meat and cook until meat is brown about 6 minutes.
4. Add red pepper, ginger, soy sauce, and stevia. Stir for 2 minutes.
5. Garnish with green onion and serve.

Nutritional Value (Amount per Serving):

- Calories 261
- Fat 10.7 g
- Carbohydrates 4 g
- Sugar 1.8 g
- Protein 35.5 g
- Cholesterol 101 mg

Easy Picadillo

Preparation Time: 10 minutes
Cooking Time: 20 minutes
Serve: 6

Ingredients:

- 2 lbs ground beef
- 1/2 cup olives
- 1 tsp ground cumin
- 1 bell pepper, diced
- 1/2 cup green onion, chopped
- 14 oz can roasted tomatoes, blended
- 2 cups grape tomatoes, halved
- 1 tbsp olive oil
- 1 tsp salt

Directions:

1. Preheat the griddle to medium heat.
2. Add oil to the griddle top.
3. Add meat and cook until browned. Season with pepper and salt.
4. Add tomatoes, cumin, green onion, and bell pepper and cook for 10 minutes.
5. Add olives and cook for 5 minutes.
6. Serve and enjoy.

Nutritional Value (Amount per Serving):

- Calories 350
- Fat 13 g
- Carbohydrates 8 g
- Sugar 4 g
- Protein 47 g
- Cholesterol 135 mg

Italian Pork Chops

Preparation Time: 10 minutes
Cooking Time: 10 minutes
Serve: 8

Ingredients:

- 8 pork chops, boneless
- 1/4 cup olive oil
- 1 tsp ground mustard
- 2 tsp garlic powder
- 2 tsp onion powder
- 4 tsp dried oregano
- 2 tbsp Worcestershire sauce
- 3 tbsp fresh lemon juice
- Pepper
- Salt

Directions:

1. Whisk oil, garlic powder, onion powder, oregano, Worcestershire sauce, lemon juice, mustard, pepper, and salt.
2. Place pork chops in the zip-lock bag then pour marinade over pork chops. Seal bag and place in the refrigerator overnight.
3. Preheat the griddle to high heat.
4. Place pork chops on hot griddle and cook for 3-4 minutes on each side.
5. Serve and enjoy.

Nutritional Value (Amount per Serving):

- Calories 325
- Fat 26.5 g
- Carbohydrates 2.5 g
- Sugar 1.3 g
- Protein 18 g
- Cholesterol 69 mg

Chapter 5: Fish & Seafood

Simple Salmon Patties

Preparation Time: 10 minutes
Cooking Time: 10 minutes
Serve: 2

Ingredients:

- 8 oz salmon fillet, minced
- 1 egg, lightly beaten
- 1/4 tsp garlic powder
- Pepper
- Salt

Directions:

1. Add all ingredients into the bowl and mix until just combined.
2. Preheat the griddle to medium-high heat.
3. Spray griddle top with cooking spray.
4. Make patties from the salmon mixture and place onto the hot griddle top and cook for 3-5 minutes on each side.
5. Serve and enjoy.

Nutritional Value (Amount per Serving):

- Calories 185
- Fat 9.2 g
- Carbohydrates 0.5 g
- Sugar 0.3 g
- Protein 24.8 g
- Cholesterol 132 mg

Mustard Tuna Patties

Preparation Time: 10 minutes
Cooking Time: 10 minutes
Serve: 4

Ingredients:

- 1 egg, lightly beaten
- 8 oz can tuna, drained
- 1 tbsp mustard
- 1/4 cup almond flour
- Pepper
- Salt

Directions:

1. Add all ingredients into the large bowl and mix until just combined.
2. Preheat the griddle to high heat.
3. Spray griddle top with cooking spray.
4. Make patties from mixture and place onto the hot griddle top and cook for 3-5 minutes on each side.
5. Serve and enjoy.

Nutritional Value (Amount per Serving):

- Calories 105
- Fat 3.2 g
- Carbohydrates 1.5 g
- Sugar 0.3 g
- Protein 16.9 g
- Cholesterol 58 mg

Mahi Mahi Fish Fillets

Preparation Time: 10 minutes
Cooking Time: 10 minutes
Serve: 3

Ingredients:

- 3 Mahi Mahi fillets
- 1 tsp paprika
- 2 tbsp fresh lemon juice
- 1 tsp cumin
- 1 tsp dried oregano
- 1/8 tsp cayenne pepper
- 3 tbsp olive oil
- 1/2 tsp onion powder
- 1/2 tsp garlic powder
- 1/4 tsp pepper
- 1/2 tsp salt

Directions:

1. Preheat the griddle to medium-high heat.
2. In a small bowl, mix together spices.
3. Brush fish fillets with oil. Sprinkle with the spice mixture and place onto the hot griddle top and cook for 4-5 minutes per side.
4. Drizzle with lemon juice and serve.

Nutritional Value (Amount per Serving):

- Calories 220
- Fat 15.3 g
- Carbohydrates 2.1 g
- Sugar 0.6 g
- Protein 19.4 g
- Cholesterol 86 mg

Easy & Tasty Salmon

Preparation Time: 10 minutes
Cooking Time: 12 minutes
Serve: 4

Ingredients:

- 4 salmon fillets
- 2 tsp black pepper
- 2 tbsp olive oil
- 2 tsp kosher salt

Directions:

1. Preheat the griddle to high heat.
2. Brush salmon fillets with oil and season with pepper and salt.
3. Place salmon fillets on hot griddle top and cook for 6-8 minutes.
4. Flip salmon fillets, covered, and cook for 2-4 minutes more.
5. Serve and enjoy.

Nutritional Value (Amount per Serving):

- Calories 295
- Fat 18 g
- Carbohydrates 0.7 g
- Sugar 0 g
- Protein 34.6 g
- Cholesterol 78 mg

Spicy Shrimp

Preparation Time: 10 minutes
Cooking Time: 4 minutes
Serve: 6

Ingredients:

- 2 lbs shrimp, peeled and deveined
- 1 tbsp chili paste
- 1 tbsp ketchup, sugar-free
- 4 tbsp sesame oil
- 1/3 cup olive oil
- 2 tbsp garlic, minced
- 2 tbsp hot sauce
- 4 tbsp fresh parsley, chopped
- 3 tbsp fresh lemon juice
- 1 tsp pepper
- 1 tsp salt

Directions:

1. In a bowl, whisk olive oil, lemon juice, chili paste, ketchup, garlic, hot sauce, parsley, sesame oil, pepper, and salt.
2. Add shrimp into the zip-lock bag then pour marinade over shrimp. Seal bag, shake well and place in the fridge for 2 hours.
3. Preheat the griddle to high heat.
4. Thread marinated shrimp onto the skewers.
5. Place shrimp skewers on a hot griddle top and cook for 2 minutes per side.
6. Serve and enjoy.

Nutritional Value (Amount per Serving):

- Calories 375
- Fat 23 g
- Carbohydrates 5 g
- Sugar 1.5 g
- Protein 35 g
- Cholesterol 319 mg

Cajun Shrimp Skewers

Preparation Time: 10 minutes
Cooking Time: 6 minutes
Serve: 4

Ingredients:

- 1 lb shrimp, shelled and deveined
- 1 tbsp fresh lemon juice
- 1 tbsp Cajun seasoning
- 2 garlic cloves, chopped
- 2 tbsp butter, melted

Directions:

1. In a small bowl, mix butter, lemon juice, and garlic. Set aside.
2. Preheat the griddle to medium-high heat.
3. Season shrimp with Cajun seasoning and thread onto the skewers.
4. Place skewers on hot griddle and cooks for 2-3 minutes per side.
5. Brush shrimp with melted butter mixture.
6. Serve and enjoy.

Nutritional Value (Amount per Serving):

- Calories 190
- Fat 7.7 g
- Carbohydrates 2.3 g
- Sugar 0.1 g
- Protein 26.1 g
- Cholesterol 254 mg

Lemon Garlic Halibut

Preparation Time: 10 minutes
Cooking Time: 14 minutes
Serve: 4

Ingredients:

- 4 halibut steaks
- 1/2 tsp Rosemary, chopped
- 2 tbsp fresh lemon juice
- 4 garlic cloves, minced
- 1/2 tsp fresh thyme
- 1/3 cup olive oil
- 1/2 tsp black pepper
- 1 tsp sea salt

Directions:

1. In a small bowl, mix together oil, thyme, rosemary, lemon juice, and garlic and set aside.
2. Place halibut steaks into the bowl.
3. Pour oil mixture on top of halibut steaks and coat well. Cover and place in the fridge for 30 minutes.
4. Preheat the griddle to medium-high heat.
5. Remove halibut steaks from the fridge and season with pepper and salt.
6. Place halibut steaks on hot griddle top and cook for 5-7 minutes.
7. Flip steaks and cook for 5-7 minutes more.
8. Serve and enjoy.

Nutritional Value (Amount per Serving):

- Calories 185
- Fat 17 g
- Carbohydrates 1.5 g
- Sugar 0.2 g
- Protein 6.1 g
- Cholesterol 11 mg

Tasty Tuna Cakes

Preparation Time: 10 minutes
Cooking Time: 10 minutes
Serve: 4

Ingredients:

- 14 oz can tuna, drained
- 1/2 cup fresh cilantro, minced
- 2 tbsp olive oil
- 1/2 tsp ground cumin
- 1/2 tsp garlic powder
- 1/2 lemon juice
- 1 egg, lightly beaten
- 1 jalapeno pepper, diced
- 1/4 cup almond flour
- 1/4 cup yogurt
- Pepper
- Salt

Directions:

1. Add all ingredients except oil into the large bowl and mix until just combined.
2. Preheat the griddle to high heat.
3. Add oil to the griddle top.
4. Make patties from tuna mixture and place them onto the hot griddle top and cook for 5 minutes.
5. Flip patties and cook for 5 minutes more.
6. Serve and enjoy.

Nutritional Value (Amount per Serving):

- Calories 215
- Fat 10.1 g
- Carbohydrates 2.3 g
- Sugar 1.6 g
- Protein 28.2 g
- Cholesterol 72 mg

Greek Tuna Patties

Preparation Time: 10 minutes
Cooking Time: 10 minutes
Serve: 6

Ingredients:

- 14 oz can tuna
- 2 garlic clove, minced
- 3 tbsp olive oil
- 1/2 tsp lemon zest
- 1 tsp dried oregano
- 2 tbsp fresh mint, chopped
- 1 tbsp lemon juice
- 2 tbsp green onions, minced
- 3 tbsp flax meal
- 1/2 cup feta cheese, crumbled
- 1 egg, lightly beaten
- Pepper
- Salt

Directions:

1. Add all ingredients except olive oil into the large bowl and mix until well combined.
2. Preheat the griddle to medium heat.
3. Add oil to the griddle top.
4. Make patties from tuna mixture and place on hot griddle top and cook patties for 5-6 minutes. Turn patties and cook for 3 minutes more.
5. Serve and enjoy.

Nutritional Value (Amount per Serving):

- Calories 200
- Fat 12.2 g
- Carbohydrates 2.3 g

- Sugar 0.7 g
- Protein 20.5 g
- Cholesterol 58 mg

Sauteed Shrimp

Preparation Time: 10 minutes
Cooking Time: 5 minutes
Serve: 4

Ingredients:

- 1 lb shrimp
- 4 tbsp butter
- 1 lemon juice
- 1/2 tsp paprika
- 1/4 tsp pepper
- 1 tsp Italian seasoning
- 1/2 tsp salt

Directions:

1. In a bowl, add shrimp, paprika, Italian seasoning, pepper, and salt. Toss well.
2. Preheat the griddle to high heat.
3. Melt butter on top of the griddle.
4. Add shrimp on top of the griddle and cook for 2-3 minutes on each side.
5. Drizzle lemon juice over shrimp.
6. Serve and enjoy.

Nutritional Value (Amount per Serving):

- Calories 245
- Fat 13.9 g
- Carbohydrates 2.3 g
- Sugar 0.4 g
- Protein 26.1 g
- Cholesterol 270 mg

Chapter 6: Vegetables & Side Dishes

Mushrooms & Green Beans

Preparation Time: 10 minutes
Cooking Time: 16 minutes
Serve: 6

Ingredients:

- 1 lb green beans, cut into 1-inch pieces
- 6.5 oz can mushroom, drained
- 1/2 cup dry white wine
- 1 1/2 tsp garlic, minced
- 2 tbsp olive oil
- 1 tsp dried thyme
- 2 tbsp sun-dried tomatoes, chopped
- Pepper
- Salt

Directions:

1. Add green beans into the boiling water and cook for 4-5 minutes. Drain well and let it cool.
2. Preheat the griddle to medium-high heat.
3. Add oil to the hot griddle top.
4. Add garlic and sauté for 1 minute.
5. Add thyme, tomatoes, mushrooms, and wine and stir well and cook for 2 minutes.
6. Add green beans and sauté for 1 minute. Season with pepper and salt.
7. Serve and enjoy.

Nutritional Value (Amount per Serving):

- Calories 90
- Fat 4.9 g
- Carbohydrates 8 g
- Sugar 1.9 g
- Protein 2.1g
- Cholesterol 8 mg

Mushroom Cauliflower Rice

Preparation Time: 10 minutes
Cooking Time: 15 minutes
Serve: 4

Ingredients:

- 10 oz cauliflower rice
- 2 garlic cloves
- 1/2 cup onion, chopped
- 1 tbsp olive oil
- 1 tbsp soy sauce
- 2 cups spinach
- 3 cups mushrooms, sliced

Directions:

1. Cook cauliflower rice according to the packet instructions.
2. Preheat the griddle to medium heat.
3. Add oil to the hot griddle top.
4. Add onion and sauté until onion is softened.
5. Add mushrooms and sauté until cooked.
6. Add garlic and sauté for a minute.
7. Add soy sauce and cauliflower rice and stir well and cook for 1-2 minutes.
8. Add spinach and cook until spinach is wilted.
9. Serve and enjoy.

Nutritional Value (Amount per Serving):

- Calories 95
- Fat 5 g
- Carbohydrates 9.2 g
- Sugar 4.5 g
- Protein 5.4 g
- Cholesterol 0 mg

Sauteed Zucchini

Preparation Time: 10 minutes
Cooking Time: 10 minutes
Serve: 4

Ingredients:

- 16 oz zucchini, chopped
- 1 tbsp olive oil
- 1/2 tsp garlic powder
- 1 tsp dried basil
- 1 tsp dried parsley
- 1 tbsp red wine vinegar
- Pepper
- Salt

Directions:

1. Preheat the griddle to medium-high heat.
2. Add zucchini and remaining ingredients into the bowl and toss well.
3. Add zucchini mixture on the hot griddle top. Cover and cook for 2-3 minutes.
4. Stir zucchini mixture and cook for 2-3 minutes more.
5. Serve and enjoy.

Nutritional Value (Amount per Serving):

- Calories 50
- Fat 3.7 g
- Carbohydrates 4.1 g
- Sugar 2.1 g
- Protein 1.5 g
- Cholesterol 0 mg

Tasty Cauliflower Wedges

Preparation Time: 10 minutes
Cooking Time: 20 minutes
Serve: 8

Ingredients:

- 1 large cauliflower head, cut into 8 wedges
- 2 tbsp olive oil
- 1/2 tsp red pepper flakes
- 1/2 tsp ground turmeric

Directions:

1. Preheat the griddle to medium-high heat.
2. Brush cauliflower wedges with oil and sprinkle with turmeric and red pepper flakes.
3. Place cauliflower wedges on a hot griddle top. Cover and cook for 8-10 minutes on each side.
4. Serve and enjoy.

Nutritional Value (Amount per Serving):

- Calories 55
- Fat 3.6 g
- Carbohydrates 5.7 g
- Sugar 2.5 g
- Protein 2.1 g
- Cholesterol 0 mg

Brussel Sprouts Skewers

Preparation Time: 10 minutes
Cooking Time: 10 minutes
Serve: 8

Ingredients:

- 24 Brussels sprouts, trimmed and cut into half
- 2 tbsp balsamic vinegar
- 1/4 cup olive oil
- 1/4 tsp garlic powder
- 1/4 tsp pepper
- 1/2 tsp salt

Directions:

1. Preheat the griddle to medium-high heat.
2. Season Brussels sprouts with garlic powder, pepper, and salt and brush with olive oil.
3. Thread Brussels sprouts onto the skewers and place skewers onto the hot griddle top and cooks for 5 minutes on each side.
4. Transfer skewers to a plate and drizzle with balsamic vinegar.
5. Serve and enjoy.

Nutritional Value (Amount per Serving):

- Calories 80
- Fat 6.5 g
- Carbohydrates 5.3 g
- Sugar 1.3 g
- Protein 2 g
- Cholesterol 0 mg

Lemon Zucchini Stir Fry

Preparation Time: 10 minutes
Cooking Time: 5 minutes
Serve:

Ingredients:

- 2 medium zucchinis, chopped
- 1 green onion, green part only, chopped
- 1 tbsp olive oil
- 1 tbsp fresh lemon juice
- Pepper
- Salt

Directions:

1. Preheat the griddle to medium-high heat.
2. Add oil to the hot griddle top.
3. Add zucchini and sauté for 3-5 minutes. Season with pepper and salt.
4. Stir in lemon juice and green onion.
5. Serve and enjoy.

Nutritional Value (Amount per Serving):

- Calories 95
- Fat 7.4 g
- Carbohydrates 7.3 g
- Sugar 3.7 g
- Protein 2.6 g
- Cholesterol 0 mg

Veggie Tofu Stir Fry

Preparation Time: 10 minutes
Cooking Time: 5 minutes
Serve: 3

Ingredients:

- 8 oz extra firm tofu, pressed and cut into cubes
- 1/4 cup onion, chopped
- 4 cherry tomatoes, chopped
- 4 cups baby spinach
- 1 tsp coconut aminos
- 3 tsp nutritional yeast
- 1/4 cup button mushrooms, chopped

Directions:

1. Preheat the griddle to medium heat.
2. Spray griddle top with cooking spray.
3. Add mushrooms and onion and sauté until onions are softened about 2-3 minutes.
4. Add tofu and stir well and cook for 1-2 minutes.
5. Add liquid aminos and nutritional yeast and stir well.
6. Add tomatoes and spinach and cook for 3-4 minutes.
7. Serve and enjoy.

Nutritional Value (Amount per Serving):

- Calories 90
- Fat 3.6 g
- Carbohydrates 8.1 g
- Sugar 1.1 g
- Protein 9.7 g
- Cholesterol 0 mg

Healthy Spinach Cauliflower Rice

Preparation Time: 5 minutes
Cooking Time: 10 minutes
Serve: 4

Ingredients:

- 4 cups cauliflower rice
- 1/4 cup vegetable broth
- 1/4 tsp chili powder
- 1 tsp garlic, minced
- 5 oz baby spinach
- 1 fresh lime juice
- 3 tbsp butter
- Pepper
- Salt

Directions:

1. Preheat the griddle to high heat.
2. Melt butter on the hot griddle top.
3. Add garlic and sauté for 30 seconds.
4. Add cauliflower rice, chili powder, pepper, and salt and cook for 2 minutes.
5. Add broth and lime juice and stir well.
6. Add spinach and stir until spinach is wilted.
7. Serve and enjoy.

Nutritional Value (Amount per Serving):

- Calories 145
- Fat 10.7 g
- Carbohydrates 9.3 g
- Sugar 4.4 g
- Protein 5.4 g
- Cholesterol 23 mg

Mushrooms & Asparagus

Preparation Time: 10 minutes
Cooking Time: 5 minutes
Serve: 4

Ingredients:

- 1 lb asparagus, trimmed and cut into pieces
- 3 tbsp butter
- 1/4 cup water
- 10 mushrooms, cleaned & sliced
- Pepper
- Salt

Directions:

1. Preheat the griddle to medium heat.
2. Melt butter on the hot griddle top.
3. Add mushroom and sauté for 1-2 minutes.
4. Transfer mushrooms on a plate.
5. Add asparagus and cook for 2 minutes.
6. Return mushrooms on hot griddle top and stir for 1 minute. Season with pepper and salt.
7. Stir and serve.

Nutritional Value (Amount per Serving):

- Calories 110
- Fat 9 g
- Carbohydrates 5 g
- Sugar 3 g
- Protein 4 g
- Cholesterol 25 mg

Zucchini Noodles

Preparation Time: 10 minutes
Cooking Time: 5 minutes
Serve: 4

Ingredients:

- 4 zucchini, spiralized
- 1/2 tbsp sesame seeds
- 2 tbsp onion, minced
- 1 tbsp soy sauce
- 2 tbsp olive oil

Directions:

1. Preheat the griddle to medium heat.
2. Add oil to the hot griddle top.
3. Add onion and sauté for 2 minutes.
4. Add zucchini noodles and cook for 2 minutes.
5. Add sesame seeds and soy sauce. Stir well and cook for 5 minutes.
6. Stir and serve.

Nutritional Value (Amount per Serving):

- Calories 105
- Fat 7.9 g
- Carbohydrates 7.6 g
- Sugar 3.7 g
- Protein 2.9 g
- Cholesterol 0 mg

Chapter 7: Snacks

Healthy Broccoli Cheese Patties

Preparation Time: 10 minutes
Cooking Time: 15 minutes
Serve: 6

Ingredients:

- 1 egg
- 4 cups broccoli florets
- 2 tbsp almond flour
- 1/4 tsp pepper
- 1/4 tsp garlic powder
- 1/4 tsp onion powder
- 3 bacon slices, cooked & chopped
- 6 tbsp cheddar cheese, shredded
- 1/4 tsp salt

Directions:

1. Add broccoli florets into the food processor and process until finely chopped.
2. Add remaining ingredients and process until well combined.
3. Preheat the griddle to high heat.
4. Make patties from broccoli mixture.
5. Spray griddle top with cooking spray.
6. Place prepared patties onto the hot griddle top and cook for 3-4 minutes on each side.
7. Serve and enjoy.

Nutritional Value (Amount per Serving):

- Calories 165
- Fat 11.9 g
- Carbohydrates 6.6 g
- Sugar 1.5 g
- Protein 9.9 g
- Cholesterol 45 mg

Cheese Broccoli Fritters

Preparation Time: 5 minutes
Cooking Time: 10 minutes
Serve: 4

Ingredients:

- 2 eggs, lightly beaten
- 3 cups broccoli florets, steam & chopped
- 2 cups cheddar cheese, shredded
- 1/4 cup almond flour
- 2 garlic cloves, minced
- Pepper
- Salt

Directions:

1. Add all ingredients into the large bowl and mix until well combined.
2. Preheat the griddle to high heat.
3. Spray griddle top with cooking spray.
4. Make patties from broccoli mixture and place onto the hot griddle top and cook until golden brown from both sides.
5. Serve and enjoy.

Nutritional Value (Amount per Serving):

- Calories 295
- Fat 22 g
- Carbohydrates 6.3 g
- Sugar 1.7 g
- Protein 19.2 g
- Cholesterol 141 mg

Cajun Broccoli Patties

Preparation Time: 10 minutes
Cooking Time: 15 minutes
Serve: 4

Ingredients:

- 2 cups broccoli florets, cooked & mashed
- 1/4 cup onion, minced
- 1 cup cheddar cheese, shredded
- 1/2 cup breadcrumbs
- 2 eggs, lightly beaten
- 1 tsp Cajun seasoning
- 1 garlic clove, minced
- 2 tbsp fresh parsley, chopped
- Pepper
- Salt

Directions:

1. Add all ingredients into the mixing bowl and mix until well combined.
2. Preheat the griddle to high heat.
3. Spray griddle top with cooking spray.
4. Make patties from mixture and place onto the hot griddle top and cook until golden brown from both sides.
5. Serve and enjoy.

Nutritional Value (Amount per Serving):

- Calories 255
- Fat 18.4 g
- Carbohydrates 9.2 g
- Sugar 2.3 g
- Protein 14.5 g
- Cholesterol 112 mg

Chicken Patties

Preparation Time: 10 minutes
Cooking Time: 15 minutes
Serve: 6

Ingredients:

- 1 lb ground chicken
- 1 tsp onion powder
- 1 tsp garlic powder
- 1 1/2 tbsp olive oil
- 3/4 cup parmesan cheese, grated
- 1 egg, lightly beaten
- 1/4 cup fresh parsley, chopped
- 1/2 tsp cayenne
- 1 tsp paprika
- 1/2 tsp salt

Directions:

1. Add all ingredients into the mixing bowl and mix until well combined.
2. Preheat the griddle to high heat.
3. Spray griddle top with cooking spray.
4. Make patties from mixture and place onto the hot griddle top and cook until golden brown from both sides.
5. Serve and enjoy.

Nutritional Value (Amount per Serving):

- Calories 225
- Fat 12.3 g
- Carbohydrates 1.6 g
- Sugar 0.4 g
- Protein 26.5 g
- Cholesterol 102 mg

Tasty Turkey Patties

Preparation Time: 10 minutes
Cooking Time: 10 minutes
Serve: 6

Ingredients:

- 1 lb ground turkey breast
- 1/2 tsp ground ginger
- 1/2 tsp garlic powder
- 1/4 cup onion, chopped
- 1 egg, lightly beaten
- 1 tbsp fish sauce
- 1 tbsp coconut amino
- 1/2 cup almond flour
- 1 tbsp olive oil
- 1/2 tsp salt

Directions:

1. Add all ingredients except oil into the mixing bowl and mix until well combined.
2. Preheat the griddle to high heat.
3. Add oil onto the hot griddle top.
4. Make patties from mixture and place onto the hot griddle top and cook for 5-6 minutes or until lightly browned from outside.
5. Serve and enjoy.

Nutritional Value (Amount per Serving):

- Calories 235
- Fat 13.1 g
- Carbohydrates 3.4 g
- Sugar 0.4 g
- Protein 29.4 g
- Cholesterol 83 mg

Parmesan Zucchini Patties

Preparation Time: 10 minutes
Cooking Time: 15 minutes
Serve: 4

Ingredients:

- 2 eggs, lightly beaten
- 2 cups zucchini, grated and squeeze out all liquid
- 1/2 cup parmesan cheese, grated
- 1/2 cup cheddar cheese, shredded
- 2 tbsp onion, minced
- Pepper
- Salt

Directions:

1. Add all ingredients into the bowl and mix until well combined.
2. Preheat the griddle to high heat.
3. Spray griddle top with cooking spray.
4. Make patties from mixture and place onto the hot griddle top and cook until golden brown from both sides.
5. Serve and enjoy.

Nutritional Value (Amount per Serving):

- Calories 101
- Fat 7 g
- Carbohydrates 3 g
- Sugar 2 g
- Protein 7 g
- Cholesterol 95 mg

Cheese Broccoli Fritters

Preparation Time: 10 minutes
Cooking Time: 12 minutes
Serve: 4

Ingredients:

- 2 egg whites
- 2 cups broccoli florets, cooked & mashed
- 1/4 cup breadcrumbs
- ¼ tsp garlic powder
- 1 cup mozzarella cheese, shredded
- Pepper
- Salt

Directions:

1. Add all ingredients in a bowl and mix until combined.
2. Preheat the griddle to high heat.
3. Spray griddle top with cooking spray.
4. Make patties from mixture and place onto the hot griddle top and cook until golden brown from both sides.
5. Serve and enjoy.

Nutritional Value (Amount per Serving):

- Calories 174
- Fat 14 g
- Carbohydrates 5 g
- Sugar 1 g
- Protein 11 g
- Cholesterol 30 mg

Italian Broccoli Fritters

Preparation Time: 10 minutes
Cooking Time: 10 minutes
Serve: 4

Ingredients:

- 8 oz broccoli florets, chopped
- 1 tsp Italian seasoning
- 1 tbsp olive oil
- 2 tbsp breadcrumbs
- 2 large eggs, beaten
- 1 cup mozzarella cheese, shredded

Directions:

1. Add all ingredients except oil in a bowl and mix until combined.
2. Preheat the griddle to high heat.
3. Add oil to the hot griddle top.
4. Make patties from mixture and place onto the hot griddle top and cook for 2-3 minutes on each side.
5. Serve and enjoy.

Nutritional Value (Amount per Serving):

- Calories 195
- Fat 14 g
- Carbohydrates 5 g
- Protein 12 g
- Sugar 2 g
- Cholesterol 125 mg

Parmesan Cauliflower Cakes

Preparation Time: 10 minutes
Cooking Time: 15 minutes
Serve: 16

Ingredients:

- 1 large egg
- 2 cups cauliflower, steamed and shredded
- 1/4 tsp onion powder
- 1/4 tsp garlic powder
- 1/2 cup parmesan cheese, shredded
- 1 tbsp butter
- Pepper
- Salt

Directions:

1. Add all ingredients into the bowl and mix until well combined.
2. Preheat the griddle to high heat.
3. Spray griddle top with cooking spray.
4. Make patties from mixture and place onto the hot griddle top and cook until golden brown from both sides.
5. Serve and enjoy.

Nutritional Value (Amount per Serving):

- Calories 16
- Fat 1 g
- Carbohydrates 0.7 g
- Protein 1 g
- Sugar 0.5 g
- Cholesterol 15 mg

Sweet Potato Patties

Preparation Time: 10 minutes
Cooking Time: 15 minutes
Serve: 6

Ingredients:

- 2 cups sweet potatoes, cooked & mashed
- 1/4 cup parsley, chopped
- 1/4 cup flour
- 2 tsp Italian seasoning
- 2 garlic cloves, minced
- 2 cups quinoa, cooked
- 1/4 cup celery, diced
- 1/4 cup scallions, chopped
- Pepper
- Salt

Directions:

1. Add all ingredients into the large bowl and mix well.
2. Preheat the griddle to high heat.
3. Spray griddle top with cooking spray.
4. Make patties from mixture and place onto the hot griddle top and cook until golden brown from both sides.
5. Serve and enjoy.

Nutritional Value (Amount per Serving):

- Calories 295
- Fat 4.1 g
- Carbohydrates 55.4 g
- Sugar 0.6 g
- Protein 9.6 g
- Cholesterol 1 mg

Chapter 8: Game Recipes

Easy & Tasty Cornish Hens

Preparation Time: 10 minutes
Cooking Time: 60 minutes
Serve: 2

Ingredients:

- 1 Cornish hen, rinse and pat dry with paper towels
- 1 tsp poultry seasoning
- 1 tbsp butter, melted
- Pepper
- Salt

Directions:

1. Brush hen with butter and season with poultry seasoning, pepper, and salt.
2. Preheat the griddle to high heat.
3. Spray griddle top with cooking spray.
4. Place hen on hot griddle top and cook for 1 hour or until the internal temperature of hens reaches 165 F.
5. Slice and serve.

Nutritional Value (Amount per Serving):

- Calories 125
- Fat 8 g
- Carbohydrates 0.5 g
- Sugar 0 g
- Protein 12 g
- Cholesterol 74 mg

Lemon Orange Cornish Hen

Preparation Time: 10 minutes
Cooking Time: 60 minutes
Serve: 2

Ingredients:

- 1 Cornish hen
- 1/4 lemon, cut into wedges
- 2 garlic cloves
- 1/4 onion, cut into chunks
- 1 1/2 fresh rosemary sprigs
- For glaze:
- 1 tbsp honey
- 1 cup of orange juice
- 1/4 fresh orange, sliced
- 1.5 oz Grand Marnier

Directions:

1. Stuff hen with lemon wedges, garlic, onions, and rosemary. Season with pepper and salt.
2. Preheat the griddle to high heat.
3. Spray griddle top with cooking spray.
4. Place hen on hot griddle top and cook for 1 hour or until the internal temperature of hens reaches 165 F.
5. Meanwhile, in a saucepan heat, all glaze ingredients until reduce by half.
6. Brush hen with glaze.
7. Slice and serve.

Nutritional Value (Amount per Serving):

- Calories 345
- Fat 10 g
- Carbohydrates 28 g
- Sugar 40.9 g
- Protein 16 g
- Cholesterol 85 mg

Delicious Cornish Hen

Preparation Time: 10 minutes
Cooking Time: 60 minutes
Serve: 2

Ingredients:

- 1 Cornish hen
- 1 1/2 tsp poultry seasoning
- 1 1/2 tsp wine
- 3 tbsp soy sauce
- 2 tbsp sugar
- 1/2 tsp pepper
- 2 cups of water
- Salt

Directions:

1. In a bowl, mix water, soy sauce, sugar, wine, poultry seasoning, pepper, and salt.
2. Place Cornish hen in the bowl and place in the fridge overnight.
3. Preheat the griddle to high heat.
4. Spray griddle top with cooking spray.
5. Remove Cornish hen from marinade and place on hot griddle top and cook for 1 hour or until internal temperature reaches 185 F.
6. Slice and serve.

Nutritional Value (Amount per Serving):

- Calories 235
- Fat 10 g
- Carbohydrates 14 g
- Sugar 12 g
- Protein 15.9 g
- Cholesterol 85 mg

Herb Cornish Hen

Preparation Time: 10 minutes
Cooking Time: 60 minutes
Serve: 2

Ingredients:

- 1 Cornish hen
- 1 tsp dried mixed herb
- 1/2 tbsp onion powder
- 1/2 tbsp smoked paprika
- 1/4 tsp pepper
- Salt

Directions:

1. In a small bowl, mix paprika, onion powder, mixed herb, pepper, and salt.
2. Rub hen with spice mixture.
3. Preheat the griddle to high heat.
4. Spray griddle top with cooking spray.
5. Place hen on hot griddle top and cook for 1 hour or until internal temperature reaches 185 F.
6. Serve and enjoy.

Nutritional Value (Amount per Serving):

- Calories 179
- Fat 10 g
- Carbohydrates 2.7 g
- Sugar 0.8 g
- Protein 15 g
- Cholesterol 85 mg

Rosemary Butter Hen

Preparation Time: 10 minutes
Cooking Time: 60 minutes
Serve: 2

Ingredients:

- 1 Cornish game hen
- 1 tsp poultry seasoning
- 1 tbsp butter, melted
- 1/2 tbsp rosemary, minced

Directions:

1. Brush hens with melted butter.
2. Mix rosemary and poultry seasoning and rub over the hen.
3. Preheat the griddle to high heat.
4. Spray griddle top with cooking spray.
5. Place hen on hot griddle top and cook for 1 hour or until internal temperature reaches 165 F.
6. Serve and enjoy.

Nutritional Value (Amount per Serving):

- Calories 219
- Fat 15 g
- Carbohydrates 0.5 g
- Sugar 0 g
- Protein 13 g
- Cholesterol 100 mg

Conclusion

If you think outdoor backyard parties, then the Blackstone outdoor gas griddle is one of the best cooking appliances available in the market. The Blackstone is one of the old and trusted griddle manufacturers popular in the USA for their outdoor griddling appliances. It is capable to cook a large quantity of food into a single cooking batch. The Blackstone griddle is available in two different sizes one is 28 inch and the other is a 36-inch model. The griddle is made up of quality stainless steel material and it comes with a black powder coating.

The book contains 80 tasty and mouth-watering griddle recipes that come from different categories like breakfast, poultry, beef, pork & seafood, vegetables & side dishes, snacks, and game recipes. The recipes written in this cookbook are unique and written into easily understandable form with their preparation and cooking time. All the recipes contain step by step instruction set which makes your cooking process easy. The recipes written in this book are ended with their nutritional value information.

CPSIA information can be obtained
at www.ICGtesting.com
Printed in the USA
LVHW021142100121
676042LV00010B/572